About the Author

Norma Watson is a woman of Black Caribbean heritage living in the United Kingdom.

She is in her 70s. A mother, a grandmother, and a great grandmother, her family plays a huge part in her life. She encourages her grandchildren to read her poems and short stories and give her their honest opinions. (At times they are unfavourable!)

Her working life has been varied. During her retirement she has been occupied with taking part in online courses on History: specialising in Black History, the roles of Black serviceman and women in the two World Wars, and The Holocaust.

NORMA WATSON

Life Through Poetry

AUSTIN MACAULEY PUBLISHERS™
LONDON • CAMBRIDGE • NEW YORK • SHARJAH

Copyright © Norma Watson 2022

The right of Norma Watson to be identified as author of this work has been asserted in accordance with sections 77 and 78 of the Copyright, Designs and Patents Act 1988.

All rights reserved. No part of this publication may be reproduced, stored in a retrieval system, or transmitted in any form or by any means, electronic, mechanical, photocopying, recording, or otherwise, without the prior permission of the publishers.

Any person who commits any unauthorised act in relation to this publication may be liable to criminal prosecution and civil claims for damages.

A CIP catalogue record for this title is available from the British Library.

ISBN 9781787103764 (Paperback)
ISBN 9781787104143 (ePub-e-book)

www.austinmacauley.com

First Published 2022
Austin Macauley Publishers Ltd
1 Canada Square
Canary Wharf
London
E14 5AA

Dedication

This book is dedicated to my granddaughter Laken Watson, whose words of encouragement carried me through the process of writing the book.

It is also dedicated to my son Stephen Watson, whose constant support is always present.

Poems

The Journey	9
My Mother......... The Other Woman	10
The Butterfly	11
Catch Me If You Can	12
Blouse and Skirt	14
Kind Black Stranger	15
1st August 1834	16
Escape	17
Black Lives Matter / Mama Don't Know	18
???	19
Nothingness	20
Adios, Amigos	21
From City to Country	22
I Do	23
Searching	24
Earth Vs Man	25
He	26
Oh, How I Wished I Had Listened	27
Youth Is Only Part-Time	28
Ageing	28
The Rose	29
Thoughts For The Future	30
The Empty Chair	31
Yesterday	32
Freedom	33
The Angel	34
You	35
Friend	36
Me	37
The Legacy	38
Tea and Biscuits	39
Sophie	40
The Puzzle	41
Whispers	42
Brown Eyes	43
Love	44
Love Me	44
The Bride	45
The Song	45
The Bench	46

The Journey

As the journey of life begins, each one takes a different path, some on the road to success, some on the road to failure, is success measured by possessions, status? Have you failed society's test whilst on your journey, no possessions, no status? Success for some is extending the hand of friendship along life's journey; failure is not trying to understand the hopelessness and sadness of some along life's journey.

At times along life's journey, we are forced to pause, give gentle guidance for those who falter. A listening ear for the troubled. For the wayward, kind words of encouragement. When life's journey ends and darkness falls, success or failure, we will all meet at the end.

My Mother......... The Other Woman

The vacant eyes which look.... which stare and ask silent questions. Who are you? What do you want? I am your child...I want you, my mother! Eyes once filled with laughter, now dulled. The face that once showed sadness, happiness, anger, now expressionless. The mother who made the rules which must be obeyed or else! The mother whose support was always there when needed, who gave unasked advice, said what she meant and meant what she said, now sits, lies, and stares.

Where are you, Mother? Who is this body which eats when fed, forgets to smile, asks no questions? Cares not for anyone or anything? The once-fierce independence now gone. The pain in your eyes as you struggle to know who I am. Please, please forgive me, Mother, I do not know you... the other woman.

Where is my once-beautiful, courageous mother, the mother who always stood up for the less fortunate who came her way, fed all, clothes recycled, a few pence given, always showed wisdom and compassion?

I thank you for the years of kindness, now only memories of you. Will I one day just sit and stare with faded memories, in silence, along life's journey? Will I become you, Mother?

KNOW WHAT? I DO NOT CARE. IF I CAN LEAVE BEHIND WHAT YOU HAVE LEFT, THEN IT IS OKAY. AH YES! YOU WILL ALWAYS BE MY PRECIOUS MOTHER AND THANK YOU.

The Butterfly

I watched you skipping happily away from me, my beautiful little butterfly, you did not look back, you had eyes only for your mummy. Yes, today is the day when you are reunited with your mummy. Your childish chatter was filled with excitement. I must be happy for you, my precious. Would it have mattered to you if you knew how my heart was breaking, yet again? The years have flown and each passing one brought joy and satisfaction; you were hard work, but it was all done with love, love that could not be measured, love that was unselfish, love that was strong and kept us going. Your childish logic brightened many a dull day. I knew one day I would have to let you go, but one day came too soon.

I must not be sad; you are such a happy child. You asked me if I missed you, and did I cry for you? I told you I did miss you, but nannies do not cry. Oh, how you dominated my life, you are everywhere. Time, which was once limited, now seems endless. All the things I wanted to do if only I had time seem shallow; the interrupted TV programmes which are now uninterrupted are dull and boring. The once-noisy house is deathly quiet, the tables remain polished.

When you came to see me, you must have seen sadness in my eyes, so once again your childish logic took over as you impatiently explained, 'You will be 100 soon, and when you die who will look after me?' Well, you are not quite right about me being almost 100 years. Then your mummy came in and your little eyes lit up. At first, we thought it would not work but we persevered together; you are so happy and confident. I must let you go to be your mummy's child. As long as life lasts, I will be here if and when needed. Thanks for the years you have given me, and my little flower that was once wilted is now blooming. Love always.

Catch Me If You Can

The time the world shook with fear, but not caused by an earthquake. Anger and wrath swept the four corners of the world and no mercy was shown to the young, the old and all races; they were struck with hate and vengeance.
The unseen enemy moved with the speed of lightning, erupting like an active volcano, as it spewed its unseen poisonous venom upon the earth.
The rich trembled, the poor wept. The sick struggle. Doctors will make choices and it won't be them. The old, sick and frail shudder. Doctors will make choices and it won't be them.

The old stay in and rely on families and friends.
The lonely stare out the window and wait for food to be left at the door by kind volunteers.
Scientific minds get together to make a cure, a cure for what? It's been given a name, 'Coronavirus'.
It dodges past them all, laughing and claiming more innocent lives as it grabs by the hundreds, squeezing until the very last breath, and goes away victorious.
The dead are left without mourners, the dying left to be comforted by strangers.

Countries compare their death toll, to see which one is in the lead.
Scientists are confused... we are all confused.
Covering the face which is frowned on by some is the new norm.
No designer wear, TOILET PAPER PLEASE!!
The whole world is united by fear.
No hiding place for man.

Services cut to the dry bones, austerity, no magic money tree, no bobbies on the beat to cut crimes.
Now bobbies on the beat walking one by one; no stop and search, stop and keep going, mate!

The free TV licence for the over 75s must go, on hold at present.
The free bus pass under threat. The buses drive by, no passengers.

Go home, we want our country back, come back.

What have we done to the world to provoke such destruction on us? We have had wars, we have killed. This is a war where no soldiers are called to fight, no guns needed.
Our only weapons are hand sanitisers, bleach and carbolic soap.
Cough into your elbow, sneeze into a tissue, do not touch your face.
No handshakes, no hugs, stay at home, if you have a home.
Keep two meters apart. Wash your hands for 20 seconds and sing 'Happy Birthday'. 'Whose birthday is it?'

Blouse and Skirt

The event was a success, the dignitaries spoke with eloquence and passion on their chosen topics.
The invited guests showed their appreciation with rapturous applause.

Food eaten. The photos taken, on observation the camera was high-tech digital, proving too sharp, every spot was highlighted.
Pencil-thin eyebrows are so, so outdated. Open pores magnified; wrinkles stood to attention. *Oil Of Dreams* has a lot to answer for!
Bingo wings were at their best, a tummy tuck would be welcomed. Then I thought I have been missed out of the photo shoot, because I could not find me.
Then with a closer look with the eye which had the cataract op I saw someone wearing my clothes. Who could that be wearing my new blouse? I should have gone to the opticians!

In utter confusion I called my son to find me. He pointed to the woman wearing my blouse!!! I had known me for 70+years, my son had known me for almost 50 years: how could I not know me?? Ha, there must be another blouse like mine.
Unsure, I asked my granddaughter to show me, me. She pointed to the woman wearing my blouse! She had only known me for 30 years, and I have known me for 70+years.
Then I thought *Best Wear* had lied when they said it was a sample and only one was made.

I put my new glasses on, closed my eye which had had the cataract op and looked through the eye which needs the cataract op: clear as crystal, that woman was wearing my blouse and my new skirt!! So, it must be me, and it was me!!

Kind Black Stranger

PAIN, PAIN, the quiet whimper, no strength to cry, the aching swollen joints, the aching head, the yellow eyes which beg silently for help, help which a mother cannot give. When will it end? please, please make it stop. You can't be touched, each joint has its own degree of intense excruciating pain. Where can I touch you? How can you be comforted? He is a child, dear God, where are you? Are you having a day off? Why choose today? The only comfort is morphine. Blood is needed, which black person will volunteer? Please, please.

Blood is on the way! And plenty is needed, and quickly.

Doctors know this is your only chance of survival. Your blood count is dangerously low. Will the tired veins be able to cope, yet again? We must find a vein!!. Doctors and nurses diligently did their work as I stood by, helpless: is this the end? So, soon you are nowhere near three score and ten. The tired weak body groans but offers no resistance when a vein is sought. Eyes closed, no longer seeking help from me. The heaving chest shows the rapidly beating heart.
Slowly, slowly as the precious red liquid enters your body, gradually the colour comes back to your face. You lie still... what blessed relief.

I do not know you; I will never meet you, but kind black stranger, THANKS, and until the next time we will need you. You see, that's how Sickle Cell goes. God came back that day.

1st August 1834

EMANCIPATION!!
FREEDOM!!
CELEBRATION!!
CARNIVAL!!

Who shall I be, Rosa Parks, Mary Seacole, African Prince, Bob Marley?
So many to choose from... footsteps through history.
Alas! No one wants to be a slave! Why? We are all free! Are we free?
The chains may not be visible. The slaves bonded because they were chained together and in the same boat sharing the sweat, the tears, the pain, the fear of the unknown, the strange faces, strange languages, the loss of dignity.

Forced to change their names; do we not change our names freely for the cause of love?
When they fought to keep theirs and stood proud. Forced to change their ways of dressing; we chose to follow fashion. Forced to change their languages; we have accepted a language when they fought to keep theirs. As a people still bound by the INVISIBLE chains.
We are still slaves in different boats, slaves without the bonding.

The stream now gone. Where giant trees once stood proudly, in their places are rows and rows of red brick houses and overhead electric cables.

Escape....

Stolen, Branded, Body oiled, show your teeth.
Auctioned to the highest bidder, vultures ready to pounce.
Separated again, no status here, the whip did the talking.

Young men used for breeding.
Our men used as tracker dogs.
Our men made to whip our own people.
Women raped; women forced to be wet nurses.
You own my body, you own my breasts, you take my milk.
Beaten and milked like a cow.
Milk for your baby, my baby left unfed.

Some say one breast for my black baby, one breast for your white baby.
Keep them separate. My black breasts are part of my black body?
My new-born baby kidnapped.
I nursed your children to whip mine and be slave masters over them.

Many of your ancestors, suckled from my black breast, when their own mothers could not or would not. My milk gave protection during infancy.

Sun-up sundown toiling in the fields, relentlessly cutting, chopping sugar cane.
Back raw from whipping. PAIN AND TEARS MUST END!!

Escape! Escape! Escape! Run, run, run to the hills, run to the mountains. Run, run for freedom!

Fight, fight, fight for freedom. Keep your chains, keep your shackles, keep your whips.

We are African warriors!!

Same tree, different branches, same roots.

Black Lives Matter / Mama Don't Know

'Mama, why Black Lives Matter?'
'I don't know, it matters because it matters.'
'Silly answer Mama, you must know.'
'How would I know, if no one told me?'
'Mama, did your mama not tell you?'
'No, my mama did not tell me, nor did her mama.'

'Teacher, why Black Lives Matter?'
'I do not know. I am teaching from the Curriculum.'
'What is the Curriculum, teacher?'
'The curriculum is set by the educated governing bodies what should be taught at schools.'

'Pastor, why Black Lives Matter?'
'We are all God's children!'

'Mama, you don't know why Black Lives Matter, teacher don't know why Black Lives Matter, Pastor don't know why Black Lives Matter; how will I know why Black Lives Matter?'

'Papa why Black Lives Matter?'
'Come sit on my knees. In the second largest and oldest continent named Africa...'
'Papa hahaha... Is that the place they walked naked?'
'No, not they, our forefathers, our ancestors. The Black race are from Africa.'
'Why did they leave Africa? Sorry, Papa, why did our ancestors leave Africa?'
'They were stolen from their homes, families and friends.'
'Stolen, Papa? But we will get in trouble if we steal. It's wrong. Did they get in trouble?'
'No, they were paid. They didn't think Black Lives Mattered. We must know our history to be proud of who we are. We know Black Lives Matter. We are Black and our lives matter.'
'Tell me more, Papa.'
'PAPA KNOWS!!!'

???

I know your history.
Do you know mine?
I know of your Kings and Queens.
Would you like to know about mine?

Oh yes, I know your history, not much to know anyway...
I'll talk as I walk.
People forced into ships, yes?
The place was Africa, a continent.
Some brave men sailed from all over the world and captured some of the
Africans, put them on board ships.
Also, some were exchanged for beads and little bits –
I suppose now that would be called bric-a-brac.
Mind, a lot died on the journey to the West Indies,
But they only went back to capture more. Ah yes, families were separated,
Young men taken,
But these things happen.
We were creating an Empire.
And, as they say,
The rest is History.
That is it, must dash!
Oops, just missed the green light.

Please, wait!!
I have lots to tell,
Who will listen?
Who will be told of inventions and inventors?
Who will learn of achievers past and present?
Scientists, adventurers, writers, poets, pioneers,
The real McCoy!
I know your history,
I was taught your history,
And you do not know mine.

Nothingness...

The roof of the world was a colour of pale blue. The creator chose the colour with expertise, confidence, and love. The sun rested in the east as if half-asleep. Beneath stood the trees, leaves of bright green gently waving to unseen friends. The stillness could be felt.

The rows of houses structurally are identical, until peering through each window the individual styles were visible. Drapes, curtains, nets, voile, Roman blinds, vertical blinds, Venetian and roller blinds; each blind tells of their origin.

An old car drove by slowly with weariness and unwillingness, seemingly on the last journey. The white van sped by with an air of urgency. A solitary pedestrian strolled by, clutching his phone for companionship and wearing a mask, a mask for protection. Echoes of a dog barking in the distance.

Standing by the door, the warm sunshine on my face. I waited and waited for the stillness to end, but there was only NOTHINGNESS...
Locked down
Locked up
Locked in... the only key is a VACCINE.

Adios, Amigos

Thirty years of, drilling, pulling, filling,
cleaning, whitening, straightening crooked teeth.
Braces on, braces off.
A daily dose of halitosis.
Screaming children with mouths filled with rotting teeth,
leaving toothless, parents looking accusingly for hurting their
overindulged children when they have fed them with bags of sweets.
Today it all ends. Gathering all the tools and carefully wrapping them
in layers of newspapers tied together with strings, travelled to the tip
furthest from home and joyfully chucked them in the skip.
'Adios, Amigos.'

From City to Country

A child of ten years old running through the fields, no fear of cars, six weeks away from school.
Bath time? A quick dip in a stream, what bliss!
Water is fetched daily from a spring.
A pit latrine, squares of newspaper on a string.

A small cottage, walls made with wattle and daub.
The only light at night an oil lamp, which also served as a centrepiece, stood on a sturdy wooden table.

Endless trees of all shapes and sizes. Trees which served as shades and never flinched
in the blazing sun, a welcomed umbrella for a sudden downpour of rain.
A carpet of buttercups beneath.
Trees which bore fruits, trees standing barren, fruitless. Trees with roots like the
feet of giants cemented in the ground.

As the day ends the sun heads west and appears less fearsome once in the distance as
it rests in visible colours of red, yellow, and orange.
In the darkness of the night the sky is lit by the full moon and an abundance of twinkling stars which at times playfully dart across the sky.

The closeness of family is felt, as uncles, aunts, and cousins gathered to listen to made-up stories, and guessed at riddles.

Each night an old man and an old lady, heads bowed, gave thanks for the blessings of the day.
Grandma and Grandpa.

Now an adult walking through lanes which were once fields.

The little cottage made from wattle and daub which was a family home, now gone serves as a resting place for the old man and the old lady,
Grandma and Grandpa
laid to rest side by side.

Memories can be told, cannot be felt, cannot be touched, now lives in the memory of a child in the body of an adult.

I Do

The cold hands of fear clutched my heart, the speed of blood rushed through my veins like a burst dam. My head throbbed, my brain tries to comprehend, my heart beats like a bass drum, BOOM!! BOOM!! BOOM!! making a thunderous CLAP! with each beat, nerves tingling throughout, my body shaking like leaves on a windy day.

My son smiled; my granddaughter smiled. My friends smiled, I smiled. Then the wait, wait, wait starts all because of a lump which should not be there. Shaking hands still writes, trembling lips still smile.

The world still spins, it is uncaring, uncaring one of its passengers could fall off. Mother Nature carries on her tasks. Hurricanes, floods, landslides, earthquakes, she cares not for one of her passengers slipping off. The sun will shine without you, the rain will continue to fall. Seasons come and go without a care or thought for a missing passenger.

Brexit In or Out, don't give a damn!

Words carefully chosen, said, 'It will have to go', but we have been together for at least 63 years! If you want another 20 years, it will have to go! So for the third time I said, 'I DO,' and he did.

Searching

I miss you, my companion and best twin friend, we have done everything together for over 65 years.

We had a farewell party for you, but farewell does not mean you are forgotten. Memories of us being together still creates a picture of us in my mind.

Mother Nature shows beauty and growth and at times anger. Is there a Father Nature hidden, who sometimes raises his head in ugliness and disaster?

Once we stood together firm and pert, doing justice to each garment which was worn; now where you once stood proud, all signs of you are gone, as if you never existed, the only sign is a scar.

I lie awake thinking, were they kind to you, or you were just another one? But I must remember you were not well and could turn against me, your friend and companion. It was not your fault; you were a pawn in the game of life.

The choice was made, you had to go to save a life.
I now sag wearily and plod along, missing you, searching, searching to find your equal which will never be found, too large, too small, uncomfortable. We have been through childbirths, romances, broken hearts, and fashions, you were always there.

Now still alone and must make do with a substitute and a second chance at life, you paid the price.

So long, MY BEST TWIN FRIEND!!!

Earth Vs Man

DESTRUCTION
POLLUTION
DESECRATION

Earth weeps and mourns for her lost trees.
Earth weeps and mourns for the wanton destruction caused by man.
Earth weeps and mourns for the desecration of rainforests caused by man.
Earth weeps and mourns for her polluted rivers, seas and oceans caused by man.
Earth weeps and mourns for her melting snow-capped mountains caused by man.
Earth weeps and mourns for her beautiful animals, captured, caged, loss of freedom.
To hunt for food, food thrown in their cages, snared, trapped, and killed for their own body parts caused by man.
Earth weeps and mourns for her lost sons and daughters of wars caused by man.

Earth weeps and mourns for her children harmed and maimed by poisonous gasses caused by man.
Earth weeps and mourns as she is repeatedly raped by man.

Earth stops weeping and mourning.

Man, now trapped in their homes like caged animals staring through windows, windows are now unseen bars, food left by the door.

EARTH TAKES VENGEANCE!!

He

He sits by the exit of the shopping centre, legs crossed and covered with a worn blanket
Which has been a constant companion over the years providing warmth and seems to be his only friend.
His hat which had seen better days sat on his head at an angle.
He looks up with eyes as blue as the sky on a summer's day.
His face darkened from the sunlight and etched with fear, sadness, and uncertainty.
His mouth toothless.
Shoppers hurried by trollies piled high, PANIC-buying again.
An outstretched hand, fingers topped with dirty nails, his feeble voice asks,
'Any change?' 'No, sorry.'

Whose husband, is he?
Whose father, is he?
Whose son, is he?
Whose brother, is he?
Whose uncle, is he?
I do not know; I know HE is a man!
'Yes sir, here you are.'

Oh, How I Wished I Had Listened

Oh, how I wished I had listened when told, 'Books must be read, homework must be done, or you will regret not doing as you have been told!' Oh, how I wished I had listened to the wisdom of the old, when told, 'Your hair will thin and your waist will thicken'! Oh, how I wished I had listened when told, 'Beauty fades and dies, handsome is as handsome does.' Oh, how I wished I had listened to those who told tales of unpursued dreams because of fear. Oh, how I wished I had listened when told by the broken-hearted, 'Beware, your heart needs care.' Oh, how I wished I had listened when told, 'Flattery is meaningless words.' The heart which was once bold, is now too old to care.

Youth Is Only Part-Time

Youth, the unlined face with bright eyes, the slender structure, the mind which always asks why, when and what. The pleasure is not knowing what is next, not caring. The continuous laughter at times which is insensitive. Speech at times can be uncaring and cutting, actions senseless and daring, no thought or care for the unfed of the world. Tears are for the old and sick. Climate change? Is that when winter ends? Buy Fair Trade? Where is that sold? Put something aside for a rainy day? Oh yes, an umbrella will do!

Ageing

Age, the lined face, dull eyes, flesh which struggles against confined spaces. The mind which now knows everything and always says, 'I told you so, Yes I know, I have done it, I have been there.' Laughter which was once spontaneous is now limited, speech is now so politically correct as not to offend. How will the unfed be fed? Recycling must be done to offset climate change. The clothes now have the stamp of Fair Trade. Rainy days are here, but so unprepared, the State Pension will not do!

The Rose

I took the centre stage, but for a while, then was pulled roughly and tied to the back. No longer my beauty a topic for conversation. I did try to keep my show going; blooms now few, no longer impressed, leaves withered fall to the ground. Just talk of the compost heap for me and which beauty will take my place.
But wait! Stop! Dear Gardener, your hands are now covered with wrinkles, your shoulders stooped, you shuffle along head down, bent and grey. Stop and think. Am I the only one ready for the compost heap?

Thoughts For The Future

When I am feeling blue and feeling low,
I think about the things I have done.
The things I would like to do keeps me going
And the things I have done, keep me smiling.

The Empty Chair

You gazed at the empty chair,
Thinking of your love no longer there.
Wondering and pondering.
His voice in your head still remains.
The long years you spent together.
The struggles you faced.
The disapproving glances, but you held it together.
There are times when you thought you should have done more, said less.
But you knew, he knew.
He had your heart, it belonged to him.
The empty chair remains.

Yesterday

Yesterday I loved and I laughed.
Yesterday you held my heart.
Yesterday each heartbeat sang with love.
Yesterday the world was ours.
Yesterday my eyes were tear-free.
Yesterday was ours forever.
With one stroke of a pen, yesterday was yesterday.

Freedom

Why is it I can't be free?
To do as I want, to do as I please?
Why can't you see, I'm just being me?
I tried to hide myself in my shadow,
I've tried lots of different characters to be.
But I want to be myself,
I want to be free, to do as I please.
So now it's time to break free
Now is the time for you to stop your games
Let me be free. Let me be me.

The Angel

An angel sent from heaven above, to see a girl who had no love.
The girl lay there, all alone. Thinking about her happy home,
How it had fallen apart, she felt sad in her heart.
The angel came, took her hand,
Said to her, 'I'll take you to a promised land.'
As they flew the angel knew she would be okay.
When they came to the promised land, the angel let go of her hand.
She looked back, and smiled at the angel.
As she ran further and further away,
Into her happy land.

You

You were my strength, when I couldn't be strong.
You were there all long.
Through times of suffering and times of joy,
Times when I really couldn't say goodbye.
You gave me the strength to carry on.
You gave me hope, so I could go on
Now I'm standing so strong,
Thanks to you,
I can take the world on.

Friend

Times when you were feeling blue,
I was there to comfort you.
Through all the suffering that you went through.
I always made the time,
To sit and listened to what you said.
I never missed a word.
I kept it all in my head.
Now you're okay and not feeling blue.
There is one small problem: I have no one to talk to.

Me

The rain showed no mercy as it pelted down; the downpour was continuous, seemingly in a hurry. The sound of the thunder was likened to the roar of a wounded lion. The lightning streaked across the sky.

The heavy quilt was soaked through making it heavier, the clothes now soaked. Underneath,
this sodden pile he lies, knees close to his chin, his arms across his chest. In the foetal position, once again he was safe in his mother's womb.

The salty tears had deserted him, death seems envious.

A torch shone on the sodden heap. A voice of authority shouted, 'Move on, Move on,
you can't stay here.' He got up slowly, shivering. The journey to nowhere began.

Tired feet could no longer carry its burden, he fell journey's end.

'It is the homeless man, it is the tramp, it is the alcoholic, it is the drug addict,
get him out the road, call an ambulance. Suddenly he is surrounded by people wanting to help him. Is he dead? dead drunk more likely, has he just scored?

As the merciful darkness and oblivion took over, all these voices which labelled him.
The tramp, the alcoholic, the drug addict.
The tramp, the alcoholic, the drug addict.
The tramp, the alcoholic, the drug addict.

NO ONE KNEW ME!!

The Legacy

Some came by ships, some came by planes, that is the way the journey was made.
Some were fair, some were light brown, some were dark brown, some were black.
From the hills, from the valleys. Uptown, downtown. No island left untouched!

Men in suits with gold teeth, ladies in hats, hair straightened.
Children with tear-stained faces.
The grip firmly held.
What lies ahead? Speculation, desperation, anticipation, the aim was the same.
THE STREETS WERE PAVED WITH GOLD!!

Heathrow, Gatwick, and Southampton were kept busy with the new arrivals.
Businesses were booming.
Men on the prowl for wives, women seeking good providers.
Some found fame, some fortune, some were guests at her Majesty's pleasure,
and when gold could not be found endured sedation.
Thirty years later, the dances and house parties stopped, aching bones can no longer do the Ska and Mash potato. The Day Centre is the meeting place, the highlight of the day is meals on wheels.
Men who once had gold teeth, now have no teeth! Women who had straightened hair,
now make do or rely on the faithful wig. Voices which once sang with John Holt, cannot
keep in tune. Hands which firmly held Red Stripe Beer and white Rum, now shake as medication is given.

Pert bosoms now sag, flat bellies bulge, chairs groan with excessive weight.
Children are old, cannot cope, parents will have to go into Care Homes.

Look around, the planes and ships brought a people who left a Legacy.

SOME GOT GOLD, BUT WE ALL GOT THE SNOW!!!

Tea and Biscuits

'MOTHER! MOTHER! we have to talk.' Why are they calling me Mother, Mother, is it about the will, again? It remains the same. Is it because I wet myself sometimes?
My tired old feet will not do as it is told.

My arthritic fingers cannot grip my cup and made me spill my tea on my new frock.

'MOTHER, MOTHER, we need to talk.' Yes, you talk, and I will listen. 'Last year when Kit and I went to France, you spent two weeks at the Care Home you
said you liked being there, we are old and cannot care for you anymore.'

Here I sit in a winged-back high-chair in a semicircle, dunking biscuits in my tea.
I do not like the old people here, they pinch my sweets and hide my teeth.

Betty, from down the corridor, spends the days looking for her mother, the silly old fool...
her mother would have been over a hundred years old!

Bill lives opposite Betty, spends his days fighting a war, which has ended a long time ago;
his walking stick is used as a rifle!

Each day I look in the mirror and wonder who is looking at me, I do not know that
sad old cow! I keep looking for my face!

Betty is looking for her mom, Bill is still fighting the war which is over.
Two old ladies visit me now and then, I do not know who they are.
I am looking for my girls Kit and Kath.

Buddies we are, off we go!
Betty is looking for her mom,
Bill is fighting a war, long over,
I am looking for my face and my girls, Kit and Kath.

Good here innit?

Sophie

Name unknown, dumped in a ditch. Used for breeding.
Too exhausted to escape, you resigned yourself to your fate.
Gentle hands lifted you, you bared your teeth; is this another of your tormentors?
You have learned not to trust. Kind soothing words allayed your fears.

Still unsure, you wanted to be left alone. There you were whimpering, tail between your legs, head down, eyes downcast, you dared not to look up.
A visible scar on your back, no hair regrowth.

Gentle voices tried again. What shall we call you, Mandy? Sophie?
You looked up and
That is when we fell in love.

Big sad brown eyes, pleading, 'Please do not hurt me,' a slight wag from your tail, you
Slowly came forward, still whimpering, you let me hug you.
'Come, Sophie, welcome to your new home.'

The Puzzle

On the table lies a thousand pieces to fit together, each piece tells a story.
Each tiny piece the fragment of a broken heart.

Bold colours, Reds, Orange, Greys, Whites.
Each tiny piece represents 2 years and 270 days.

Reds——the Roses for Valentines.
Blues——the colours of the Sky and the oceans represents the height
and depth of our
love.
Orange——Watching the glow of the sunset in the warmth of your arms.
White——The purity of our love.

As each tiny piece clicks together, it remains unfinished.
YOU hold the missing piece.

Whispers

Soft whispers in the night saying, 'Do it, do it, you know you want to do it, no one will know. It will be all right.'
'Take the knife from the cupboard, be brave.'
He succumbs.

There stood the temptress, snowy white, like a bride in waiting.
Excitement at fever pitch, he took the knife, one cut, then another.
As it sank into the
moist softness, he gasped with delight at the revelation! The Chocolate Cake, triple layers of chocolate, filled with raspberry, strawberry jelly, lemon curd, his favourite. He sank his teeth in, the fillings oozed out, covering his moustache and the corners of his mouth. His fingers covered with strawberry jam, which he licked one by one, blobs of lemon curd, and strawberry jelly rested on his heaving chest.

Soft whispers: more, more, until more was no more. The sweetness remained in his mouth as a reminder.

Blissful contentment enveloped him like a blanket.
Soft whispers: 'You naughty, naughty fat man, YOU have ruined your diet!!'

Brown Eyes

Big brown eyes of a wounded child looked up; his skin stretches to cover his emaciated
body. His body malnourished; he tries to cry, can only utter a low moan.

A mother tries to breastfeed her infant, due to lack of food she could not produce milk. Breast is best they say, not for this infant.
Her gaunt face looks into the face of her child, she knows her short life is nearing the end. She has no tears to shed.

A malnourished father looks at his infant son whose skin stretches to cover his emaciated body. The only support the father can offer is to weakly brush the flies away from his son's face as they continuously zoomed over his emaciated body landing on all areas of his face, the child never flinched.

Shortly after and alone the father buried his son.
In agony his short life ends.

No child has ever started a war, no child has ever made a bomb, no child has ever made a gun.

Adults start wars, adults make guns, adults make bombs.
Innocent and blameless children are dying from wounds inflicted by adults.
Innocent and blameless children are dying malnourished, caused by the ravages of war.

Love

Two young lovers, who were never apart.
Wanted to find a path together.
To see what the future holds.
And if their love would ever fold.

So as their life carried on
They found their love was strong.

Love Me

Love me, love me until the seven seas become one.
Love me, love me until the seven oceans become one.
Love me, love me until the four corners of the earth become one.

Love me, love me with each breath you take.
Love me, love me until our beating hearts become one.

Love me, love me forever and ever.

The Bride

I wanted to be Mary in the Christmas play; I was not chosen.
I wanted to be in the school choir; I was not chosen.
I wanted to be in the band; I was not chosen.
I wanted to be a bride; you chose me.

The Song

A love song was written, it was not for me.
A dear Jane letter was written and it was for me.

The Bench

New-born baby wrinkled and red cries... such joy and happiness.
Old man wrinkled and red cries... What are you crying for, Bill...?
Your wife has been dead for 20 years.

Baby says, 'Ma, ma, da, da...' Ah bless, he will be talking soon!
Bill asks for his ma and dad... I have told you over and over, your parents have died a long, long time ago!

Baby soils his nappy... Who is a clever boy?
Old man soils his pants... oh no not again!

Baby gives his toothless grin... which is caught on camera!
Old man gives his toothless grin... Put your dentures in Bill, you won't be able to eat your dinner!

Baby takes his first wobbly steps... Come, come I will catch you if you fall.
Old man takes what might be his last wobbly steps... Sit down Bill, or you will fall and break your hip.

Baby throws his toy out the cot... You have a good aim, will play cricket one day.
old man drops his walking stick... I do not have the time to keep picking up your stick.

Baby cries and cries... Oh, you are so tired; bath and bed time. I will read you a story and sing you a lullaby.
Old man cries, 'I am tired, need to go to bed'; it's too early Bill, you can't go to bed now, you will be up all night and disturb the others.

Baby wakes and cries... Who is a hungry little boy? Feeding time!
Old man wakes and cries... What are you crying for? You are well looked after, you are seeking attention. Breakfast is an hour's time; you will have to wait.

Baby utters his first made-up words... You will be ready for school soon.
Old man mumbles and talks to himself... . I think dementia has set in.

Baby sits in his pram in the park... Strangers pass by with admiring glances and comments... You are such a beautiful baby, going to break a few hearts one day!!

Old man sits on a bench in the park, everyone passes by without a glance!

Baby boy, one day you will be the old man sitting on the bench in the park, and they will all pass by!!

CPSIA information can be obtained
at www.ICGtesting.com
Printed in the USA
LVHW082123021122
732216LV00006B/185